# BIOLOGICAL &

# CHEMICAL WARFARE

Essential Issues

# BIOLOGICAL &
# W CHEMICAL ARFARE

BY HAL MARCOVITZ

Content Consultant
Les Paldy, Distinguished Service Professor
Department of Technology and Society
State University of New York at Stony Brook

ABDO
Publishing Company

# CREDITS

Published by ABDO Publishing Company, 8000 West 78th Street, Edina, Minnesota 55439. Copyright © 2010 by Abdo Consulting Group, Inc. International copyrights reserved in all countries. No part of this book may be reproduced in any form without written permission from the publisher. The Essential Library™ is a trademark and logo of ABDO Publishing Company.

Printed in the United States of America,
North Mankato, Minnesota
102009
012010

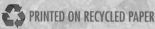 PRINTED ON RECYCLED PAPER

Editor: Mari Kesselring
Copy Editor: Paula Lewis
Interior Design and Production: Emily Love
Cover Design: Emily Love

**Library of Congress Cataloging-in-Publication Data**
Marcovitz, Hal.
  Biological & chemical warfare / Hal Marcovitz.
    p. cm. — (Essential issues)
  Includes bibliographical references.
  ISBN 978-1-60453-951-6
  1. Biological warfare—Juvenile literature. 2. Biological weapons—Juvenile literature. 3. Chemical warfare—Juvenile literature.
4. Chemical weapons—Juvenile literature. I. Title. II. Title:
Biological and chemical warfare.
  UG447.8.M317 2010
  358.3—dc22
                                        2009029947

# TABLE OF CONTENTS

*In 2001, an attacker sent deadly anthrax spores through U.S. mail.*

# THE HUNT FOR THE ANTHRAX KILLER

On September 11, 2001, terrorist attacks on the World Trade Center in New York and the Pentagon in Washington DC shook the world. But in the following weeks, Americans were shocked by another deadly and unexpected attack.

The September 11 attackers had been identified as members of the radical Islamic group al-Qaeda. But the identity of the person responsible for this second wave of terror remained a mystery. This attacker was sending deadly anthrax spores in ordinary envelopes by U.S. mail. The letters went to members of the media and political leaders in Washington DC.

Anthrax is one of dozens of biological agents that can be used as weapons. Many of these weapons have the potential to kill thousands of people. Armies have used biological and chemical agents for centuries. Weapons such as mustard gas, chlorine gas, sarin, cholera, and plague have been used to defeat enemies on the battlefield without firing a shot. Recently, terrorism has grown into a major international threat. Many people worry that terrorists will find a way to use deadly biological and chemical agents against their enemies. Biological weapons expert Barry Kellman explained, "If the objective is to inflict mass death

### Fluffy Spores

Anthrax spores are formed by the bacteria *Bacillus anthracis*. The spores are hard grains that protect the bacteria, keeping it alive for years. Together, the spores look like a white powder such as flour, confectioners' sugar, or talcum powder. "When you shake it up, it's fluffy," said William Patrick III, a former U.S. Army biological weapons expert.[1]

*A letter and anthrax spores were sent to Senator Tom Daschle.*

and panic on a mixed population . . . emerging
bioweapons offer remarkable potential."[2]

## PRIME SUSPECT

The first victim to die in the 2001 anthrax attacks
was Robert Stevens. He was an editor at a newspaper
office in Boca Raton, Florida. Traces of anthrax
spores were found on his computer keyboard, in

the newspaper's mailroom, and elsewhere in the building. Although the envelope was never found, Stevens had come into contact with the spores and ingested them. He may have touched his mouth or nose after touching the envelope. He may have simply inhaled the spores as they floated out of the envelope when he opened it.

Within days, another 21 people contracted anthrax. Four more of them died. Two of the victims were postal employees. They may have touched letters containing anthrax spores as they were sorted in a New Jersey mail center. Two other victims were women with no connection to the media or politics. They may have simply touched envelopes that came into contact with the envelopes containing the spores.

As news of the deaths was reported, law enforcement officials began a massive international investigation. But they soon found themselves struggling with a case that contained few clues. Scientists and agents from the Federal Bureau of Investigation (FBI) examined the evidence. They determined the spores were the work of an expert with access to a sophisticated lab. That meant the spores could have been developed in an enemy

## Who Were the Anthrax Victims?

The first victim of the anthrax attacks was Robert Stevens, 63. Stevens worked as a photo editor at the *Sun*. Evidently, he opened the envelope containing the anthrax spores. A mailroom worker at the newspaper also contracted anthrax but did not die.

Two U.S. Postal Service employees, 47-year-old Joseph Curseen Jr. and Thomas Morris Jr., 53, died after contracting anthrax at the postal facility in Hamilton Township, New Jersey. This was the facility that processed the letters containing anthrax.

The two other victims were Kathy Nguyen, 63, who lived in New York City and Ottilie Lundgren, 94, of Oxford, Connecticut. They simply may have handled envelopes that came into contact with the deadly envelopes.

country with a biological weapons program. The spores could have also been produced in a U.S. lab where anthrax research is conducted. One such lab is located in Frederick, Maryland, at Fort Detrick. At this lab, scientists perform research on anthrax vaccines.

By 2006, the anthrax killer still had not been found. In Washington DC, FBI Director Robert Mueller assigned a new task force to go through the old evidence to determine if anything had been missed. Soon, the task force discovered something that had been overlooked by the original investigators. In 2002, FBI scientists had collected anthrax samples from laboratories to see if any of them matched or were similar to the anthrax that had killed the victims. They hoped to find a DNA link between the anthrax in the mail and anthrax from a lab. This could lead them to the killer. At Fort Detrick, scientists worked with many different versions of anthrax. In 2002, the FBI had requested a specific kind of anthrax from the lab. Now the task force discovered that biologist Bruce Ivins had handed in a different anthrax sample than the one they had requested.

The FBI task force returned to Ivins's lab. They obtained the anthrax sample that was originally requested in 2002. Ivins immediately became a suspect in the murders.

## CLOSING IN

As FBI agents looked into Ivins's background, they found that he was a mentally unstable individual who suffered from depression and suicidal

### The Ames Strain

Bacteria like the one that causes anthrax often comes in many varieties, or strains. The Ames strain is regarded as one of the deadliest samples of anthrax ever discovered. It was this strain that Bruce Ivins allegedly used in his attacks. Samples of this strain are used in a dozen or more U.S. labs that study anthrax. At first, FBI scientists doubted whether they could make the DNA link between what they seized from Ivins's lab and the anthrax found in the bodies of the victims.

But Ivins had altered the Ames sample, which he labeled RMR-1029, mutating it to make it even more deadly. By doing so, Ivins had given the sample a unique genetic fingerprint. This made it easier for the FBI to perform the DNA link.

Scientists who later examined RMR-1029 were awed by the purity of the anthrax bacteria Ivins had been able to produce. "It was his ultimate creation," said FBI microbiologist Jason D. Bannon. "This was the culmination of a lot of hard work."[3]

thoughts. Ivins was under the care of a psychiatrist. He had also been receiving counseling by a social worker, Jean Duley, who alleged that Ivins had been threatening her. In the summer of 2008, she obtained a protection order from a judge requiring Ivins to stay away from her.

The FBI also learned that Ivins was an expert on anthrax. He was one of the few people able to produce the sophisticated quality of the anthrax that had killed the five victims. "He was a critical part of our vaccine studies," said John Ezzell, a former top scientist at Fort Detrick who worked with Ivins. "Most of the time, he was very happy and outgoing. He did good work. He was very conscientious and he worked long hours to get the work done."[4]

Meanwhile, FBI scientists found some similarities in the DNA between the anthrax that killed the victims and the anthrax seized from Ivins's lab.

**Spreading the Pestilence**

Some of Bruce Ivins's friends and coworkers suspected that he was mentally tormented. A year before his alleged crime he sent an e-mail to a friend that said, "I wish I could control the thoughts in my mind. . . . When I'm being eaten alive inside, I always try to put on a good front here and at home, so I don't spread the pestilence."[5]

By late July 2008, the FBI prepared to charge him with the murders of the five anthrax victims. Ivins knew he was a suspect. Federal agents had questioned him repeatedly. The agents had also interviewed his coworkers, neighbors, and friends. On July 28, Ivins took an overdose of prescription medicine and died.

Soon after Ivins's suicide, the FBI closed the case on the 2001 anthrax murders. Unable to determine an exact motive, they speculated that Ivins could have benefited financially from his crime. Perhaps he believed that the panic his murders caused would increase the demand for an anthrax vaccine. They also suggested that he was a mentally troubled individual who was acting out his hostility toward politicians and the press. However, some people still doubted that Ivins was guilty of the attacks.

**Targets**

Bruce Ivins allegedly sent envelopes that contained anthrax spores to two U.S. senators, Tom Daschle of South Dakota and Patrick Leahy of Vermont. He also targeted journalists at NBC News, ABC News, CBS News, the *New York Post*, and the *Sun*. The choice of victims puzzled investigators. Ivins might have felt the impact of his crime would be greater if he attacked the nation's most influential journalists. But investigators could provide few clues why the *Sun* was targeted. The *Sun* specializes in celebrity gossip and offbeat stories and usually does not take political positions.

The 2001 anthrax attacks were linked to a man who acted alone. However, biological and chemical warfare remains a major concern in the United States—and with good reason. In the past, hostile enemies have used these weapons with disastrous results. ⌐

Police talked to Bruce Ivins's wife after his suicide.

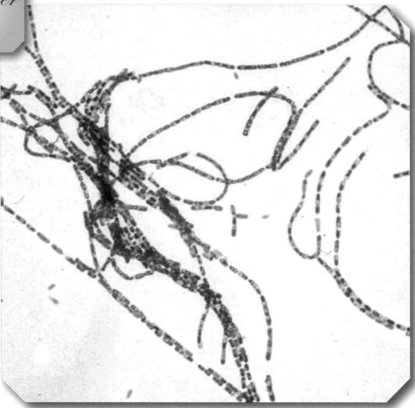

*Anthrax under a microscope*

# DEADLY WEAPONS

ozens of biological, chemical, and even radiological substances can be turned into weapons. However, these are all very different types of weapons and are created from different resources. They can be used in different ways.

## BIOLOGICAL WEAPONS

Biological weapons come from natural substances in the environment. However, they can be altered in a lab and made more deadly. Biological weapons infect a person with a dangerous disease. The disease usually progresses quickly and causes death. Many people worry that bioterrorists will develop biological weapons to create pandemics—widespread diseases that spread within the whole country or even the world. Biological weapons could be brought into the food or water supply or sent in the mail like anthrax.

## ANTHRAX

Because of the Bruce Ivins case, anthrax is widely known as a biological weapon. It is a common bacteria found among farm animals. Anthrax bacteria can live in the soil and become active when exposed to air. Many farm animals get the disease by grazing on infected ground. In 1945, an anthrax outbreak in Iran killed approximately 1 million sheep. Small but deadly epidemics have occurred in the United States too. In 2001, hundreds of farm animals in Minnesota, California, and North Dakota died due to anthrax.

Anthrax is not contagious. A person who has anthrax cannot infect another person. The disease is spread by directly touching the bacteria, ingesting the germs, or breathing in the spores. Humans can also be infected by eating meat from an infected animal. Anthrax spores can be cultured in a lab, allowing the bacterium to live indefinitely. This would make it easy for the spores to be produced in large quantities, stockpiled, and used as a weapon.

## MASS PANDEMICS

Over the course of human history, there have been at least three mass pandemics of plague. Plague is a highly contagious disease. It is caused by bacteria on rats' bodies and spread by fleas. According to the World Health Organization (WHO), approximately 3,000 cases of plague occur each year, mostly in Africa, South America, and Asia. But since industrialized countries do a good job of controlling rat populations, a new plague pandemic in the United States is unlikely. However, plague could be released as a weapon—and was during World War II. The Japanese army unleashed plague-carrying fleas over China to infect the population.

Another disease spread by insects is tularemia. Flies, ticks, and mosquitoes are known to carry the bacteria that cause this disease. A WHO study concluded that if terrorists spread 110 pounds (50 kg) of the tularemia bacteria over a city of 5 million people, some 250,000 people would be harmed. Another 19,000 people would die.

Diseases that have been mostly eliminated through vaccines can surface as new threats if they fall into the hands of enemy nations or terrorists. Over the centuries, smallpox killed an estimated 500 million people worldwide before it was virtually eliminated by a new vaccine. In fact, the vaccine was so successful in eliminating smallpox that it is no longer administered. No one in the United States has been vaccinated against smallpox since 1972. However, this means that hundreds of millions of Americans and others face infection with the deadly disease if someone finds a way to capture the smallpox virus and use it as a weapon.

### Three Types of Plague

There are three types of plague. Throughout history, bubonic plague has been the most common form. It causes fever, chills, headache, vomiting, and nausea.

Septicemia plague is when the bacteria enters the patient's bloodstream. The patient will experience symptoms similar to those of bubonic plague, but also bleeding within the skin may occur.

Pneumonic plague is the most deadly and contagious of the three forms of plague. This plague afflicts the patient's lungs and can cause respiratory failure.

**Dark Winter**

The U.S. government explored the use of smallpox as a biological weapon in a study completed in 2001 titled Dark Winter. The study speculated that if terrorists unleashed the smallpox virus on three large American cities, 1 million victims would die within the first two months of the pandemic. Another 2 million victims would suffer from the symptoms of the disease.

Two known stockpiles of smallpox virus exist in the world. One is under the control of the Centers for Disease Control and Prevention (CDC) in the United States. The virus is kept in a secret location. The other stockpile is in Russia. The smallpox virus is used in government labs for research purposes. However, intelligence officials worry that hostile countries, particularly North Korea, have obtained the smallpox virus and could use it as a weapon.

A Homeland Security Department spokesman said, "The United States is concerned that countries other than the U.S. and Russia have stockpiles of smallpox."[1]

Cholera is another disease spread by bacteria that could be used as a weapon. Cholera attacks the gastrointestinal system. It often occurs due to poor sanitary conditions. Like smallpox and plague, cholera is very rare. However, emergency preparedness officials worry that terrorists could spread cholera by tainting water and food supplies.

## CHEMICAL WEAPONS

Chemical weapons are created from chemicals. They usually harm or kill a victim very soon after exposure. These weapons have been used on the battlefield. They have also been used against citizens during war. However, in many cases, these substances are used for ordinary purposes. For example, chlorine is used to purify the water in swimming pools. But as a gas, chlorine can cause burning pain in the eyes and throat and spasms in the chest.

Unlike the material to create

### The Dangers of Chlorine Gas

Chlorine is one of the most common chemicals. For example, it is used to keep swimming pools clean. Bleach contains chlorine, too. In most homes, a bottle of bleach can be found in the laundry room, where it is used to whiten fabrics.

Huge chemical plants manufacture nothing but chlorine. Many environmental activists, as well as government officials, are concerned that terrorists could target these plants. The terrorists could attack the plants, releasing huge amounts of deadly chlorine gas. In 2001, the environmental group Greenpeace published a report about chlorine. It suggested attacks on chlorine plants in Michigan, Texas, and West Virginia would endanger the lives of nearly 600,000 people.

It is believed that even a small amount of chlorine gas would be deadly to anyone within three miles (4.8 km) of the leak. Even those within ten miles (16 km) of the leak would suffer permanent respiratory damage. Gary Bass, head of OMB Watch, an organization that strives to make government activities visible to citizens, says, "What's shocking is how few people know about dangers in their own neighborhoods."[2]

biological weapons, the material to make chemical weapons does not occur naturally. Chemical weapons are created in labs from raw materials. Most chemical weapons are used as gases. Some 70 different chemicals are known to have been used in the creation of chemical weapons. Chemical weapons fall into four groups: blister agents, blood agents, nerve agents, and pulmonary agents.

❖ Blister agents, such as mustard gas, cause severe irritation to the eyes, the skin, and the lungs. Blister agents generally do not kill, but they do cause severe debilitation. Still, death can occur from complications, particularly when the gas scars the lungs.

❖ Blood agents are poisonous gases that are absorbed by the blood. They cause seizures, respiratory failure, and cardiac arrest. During World War II, the Nazis used the blood agent Zyklon B to kill millions of concentration camp inmates.

❖ Nerve agents shut down the body's central nervous system. One common nerve agent is sarin. It can cause death within 15 minutes.

*Ambulances waited outside a theater in Moscow, Russia, after a gas was sent through the building's ventilation system.*

❖ Pulmonary agents are gases that attack the lungs. They cause choking. The most common pulmonary agent is chlorine gas.

Some of the deadly effects of gases were illustrated in 2002 when Russian soldiers stormed a theater in Moscow. The theater had been taken over by terrorists nearly three days earlier, and they held more than 700 hostages. Finally, the soldiers pumped what may have been a nerve gas into the theater's ventilation system. Inside the theater, many of the terrorists died— but so did 117 of the hostages. "It smelled of grass and ginger," said one of the

## Lethal Effect

Russian leaders have not identified the nerve agent they pumped into the Moscow theater in 2002. They label it a "combat nervous paralyzing gas."[4] Experts speculated that those who authorized the use of the gas believed that it would only knock out—not kill—the hostages and their captors. However, because the standoff had gone on for nearly three days, many of the captives were in a weakened state. Therefore, the gas killed 129 of the hostages.

survivors, Vladimir Nikolayevich. "Then I lost consciousness and woke up in an ambulance."[3] Twelve more hostages died from exposure to the gas after being removed from the theater. The Russians have never identified the gas that was used. Experts believe it was far more deadly than the Russians had anticipated.

## RADIOLOGICAL WEAPONS

Radioactive substances are commonly used in hospitals and industries, but they can be very dangerous. Typically found in chemical form, radioactive materials can be used to build a dirty bomb. A dirty bomb is officially known as a "radiological dispersion device." When exploded, the bomb would cause little physical damage. However, the vapors released by the blast could spread deadly radiation poisoning over a wide area. As of 2008, a dirty bomb had never been detonated.

In 2003, emergency responders set up a fake dirty bomb attack in Seattle, Washington, to practice for a real attack.

*U.S. nurses trained for gas attacks during World War II.*

# CENTURIES OF KILLING

Biological and chemical weapons have been used for centuries. The first use of poison gas by one army against another may have occurred during the Peloponnesian War in the fifth century BCE. Allies of the Spartans flung torches that burned sulfur and pitch over the walls of an Athenian fort. The weapon was a crude form of mustard gas.

By the fourteenth century, armies knew that people who came into contact with decaying bodies frequently became sick. They used dead horses as weapons, sending them over fortress walls. In 1340, in a siege on a French castle, attackers flung so many dead horses over the castle wall that the stench inside became unbearable. The defenders called for peace. Six years later, the Tartars employed a similar technique. Instead of horses, they used the bodies of soldiers who had died from the bubonic plague. They flung their dead over the walls of the Russian city of Caffa. The frightened defenders fled the city.

During the American Revolution in the 1770s, the British tried to infect the Continental army with smallpox. The British had recruited a group of escaped slaves by promising the slaves freedom if they fought against the colonists. Many of these former slaves became infected with smallpox, however. The British left them behind, hoping that once they died, their decaying corpses would infect the Americans. One Connecticut soldier wrote,

*These poor creatures, having no care taken of them, many [crawled] into the bushes about and died, where they lie infecting the air around them with an intolerable stench and great danger.[1]*

The strategy failed. As far back as the 1720s, doctors had developed a smallpox vaccine. Early in the war, General George Washington had ordered vaccinations for all soldiers.

## WORLD WAR I

In 1899 and 1907, several nations signed treaties called the Hague Peace Conventions. These treaties outlawed the use of chemical and biological weapons during warfare. Less than a decade after the second treaty was signed, Germany broke the pact. The Germans used mustard and chlorine gases on troops at the Second Battle of Ypres in Belgium during World War I in 1915. British soldier Anthony Hossack recalled the effects of chlorine gas he faced during the war: "One man came stumbling through our lines. [He] was frothing at the mouth, his eyes started from their sockets, and he fell writhing at the officers' feet."[2] The Germans also used anthrax to poison the livestock of the Allied armies. Soon,

the Allies would also use chemical
weapons.

It is estimated that by the end of
World War I, more than 90,000
soldiers and civilians died in gas
attacks. Another 1.2 million suffered
illnesses or injuries from chemical
warfare. Stunned by such numbers,
world leaders signed the Geneva Protocol in 1925.
This outlawed the use of chemical and biological
weapons in warfare yet again.

> "The deadly rain that fell from the aircraft made all those who touched it fly shrieking with pain."[3]
>
> —Ethiopian Emperor Haile Selassie describing Italian gas attacks on his people

## WORLD WAR II

A little more than a decade later, the Geneva
Protocol was also ignored. The Axis powers
used chemical and biological weapons during
World War II. Just prior to the war, the Italian army
conquered Ethiopia largely by dropping mustard
gas onto thousands of helpless villagers. During the
war, the Nazis used chemical agents to kill millions
of Jewish people and other concentration camp
prisoners. And the Japanese used biological agents
to kill tens of thousands of civilians in China.
Biological and chemical weapons have proved more
effective against civilians than soldiers. Soldiers are

usually equipped with protective gear to prevent them from breathing in the harmful gases.

By 1944, the Germans were bombarding London with V-1 rockets. The rockets destroyed parts of the city and took many lives. British leaders feared the Germans would load the V-1 rockets with biological weapons. To counter the V-1 attacks, British Prime Minister Winston Churchill asked the United States for half a million bombs packed with anthrax. Churchill planned to drop them on German cities.

But as it turned out, the Germans did not pack the V-1 rockets with deadly poisons. And the U.S. government resisted Churchill's request for anthrax. President Franklin D. Roosevelt had considered using chemical and biological weapons on the enemy. However, he changed his mind after receiving horrifying reports of the Axis gas attacks on civilians.

## THE VIETNAM WAR

After World War II, research into chemical and biological weapons continued for several decades. In 1969, President Richard M. Nixon suspended the military's biological and chemical weapons development program. He felt that the use of such weapons was inhumane. Still, the military continued to maintain the Fort Detrick lab to study weapons and search for antidotes and vaccines. Meanwhile, other nations also abandoned their programs.

In 1972, more than 100 nations signed the Biological and Toxin Weapons Convention. It banned the development, production, and stockpiling of biological weapons. It also reaffirmed the 1925 Geneva Protocol banning their use. It did permit research on biological materials that could be used for weapons as long as it is for medical or defensive procedures.

## The Whitecoats

During the 1950s, the U.S. military's chemical and biological weapons program lacked an important element: human guinea pigs. In 1954, 2,200 volunteers agreed to be exposed to germs that were under study. These volunteers were U.S. Army soldiers nicknamed the "Whitecoats." The men were not exposed to germs that could kill them, but many became very ill. Most of the tests were conducted in laboratories, but eventually the scientists wanted to do the tests under battlefield conditions.

Thirty Whitecoats were flown to a secluded desert in Utah in 1955. They were exposed to a cloud containing the bacteria that causes Q fever. Most of the Whitecoats contracted the disease, which caused high fever, joint pain, headache, and weakness. All were given antibiotics and recovered, though some spent a few months recovering in the hospital. One of the Whitecoats, Lloyd Long, said,

*I woke up feeling I was coming down with the worst case of flu that I ever had. My eyes were very, very sensitive to light. I wanted the room dark. I ached everywhere. I was just incredibly sick, just very, very sick.[4]*

*Airplanes sprayed defoliants on the jungles of Vietnam.*

Following the collapse of the Soviet Union, a new treaty, the 1997 Chemical Weapons Convention, banned the development, production, and stockpiling of chemical weapons. It also banned their use as required by the 1925 agreement and established strong inspection systems to make sure that nations complied with the treaty.

Although the United States suspended its weapons program in 1969, it still used chemicals to help wage war. During the Vietnam War, approximately 20 million gallons (75.7 million L) of Agent Orange and other defoliants were sprayed on the jungles of South Vietnam near U.S. military installations. These chemicals removed the leaves from trees, which destroyed some of the enemy's hideouts and sniper posts. Agent Orange included a highly toxic chemical called dioxin. Even after the war, the dioxin remained in the soil. In Vietnam, some 400,000 people who came into contact with chemical defoliants have been killed or maimed. Another 2 million people have developed cancers. Additionally, 500,000 children have been born with birth defects.

## IRAQ AND CHEMICAL WEAPONS

The Gulf War of 1991 revealed that Iraq had a chemical and biological weapons program in the past. The country had used mustard gas and sarin against rebels in the 1980s. Iraq had also used chemical weapons on enemy troops during its decade-long war with Iran.

In 2003, the United States launched a war against Iraq. President George W. Bush and other world

"I have decided that the United States of America will renounce the use of any form of deadly biological weapons that either kill or incapacitate. Mankind already carries in its own hands too many of the seeds of its own destruction."[5]

—*President Richard M. Nixon, after halting the United States' biological and chemical weapons development program*

leaders believed that Iraqi dictator Saddam Hussein
was developing chemical and biological weapons.
Some storehouses of raw chemicals that were
suspected to be components of a weapons program
were found. However, no hard evidence was found to
prove that Iraq still maintained an active program.

## POISONED INDIVIDUALS

In the early 2000s, chemical and biological
weapons were used to poison two men. In 2004,
Ukrainian political leader Viktor Yushchenko was
poisoned with dioxin in an assassination attempt.
He survived and went on to become president
of the Ukraine. Former Russian spy Alexander
V. Litvinenko did not survive a similar attempt.
In 2006, he had been critical of Russian Prime
Minister Vladimir Putin. Litvinenko died after
he was poisoned in London. Russian agents had
allegedly killed him with the radioactive substance
polonium 210. ⌐

*Viktor Yushchenko was poisoned with dioxin but survived.*

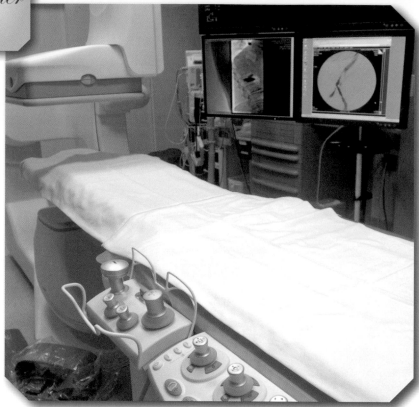

*Radiological materials can be found in X-ray equipment.*

# BIOLOGICAL AND CHEMICAL TERRORISM

nowledge and materials are required to make a biological, chemical, or radiological weapon. In some cases, these resources are easy to track down. Some experts worry that terrorists can too easily produce the deadly weapons.

In 2001, two woodsmen working in a forest in the former Soviet state of Georgia found some old metal canisters lodged in some rocks. The men touched the canisters, which gave off heat. Thinking the canisters would keep them warm overnight, the men took the canisters back to their tent. Hours later, the men stumbled into a hospital. They were suffering from burns and severe radiation sickness. The canisters contained a radioactive substance.

Scientists from the International Atomic Energy Agency (IAEA) investigated the case. They discovered the canisters had been part of a project undertaken years before by the former Soviet Union. They were meant to provide long-lasting sources of energy for remote lighthouses and airplane tracking stations. The scientists were horrified that the canisters had been so carelessly discarded.

Evidently, when the Soviet Union collapsed, those in charge of the project lost track of the canisters. Now there were perhaps hundreds of missing containers of dangerous radioactive materials strewn throughout the former Soviet states. This posed a danger to citizens like the two woodsmen who happened to find the canisters. But the discovery also worried security experts.

If these materials fell into the hands of terrorists or other enemies, they could use them to make dirty bombs.

## BUILDING A DIRTY BOMB

Some people believe a terrorist would be especially interested in building a dirty bomb. Jack Caravelli, a U.S. Energy Department spokesman, said,

> *A dirty bomb is not a nuclear weapon but a real threat . . . it is a weapon that could wreak havoc in ways far beyond its physical consequences. And that makes it an ideal terrorist weapon.*[1]

A dirty bomb would be easier for a terrorist to construct than many other weapons. It can be exploded with a single stick of dynamite. Some materials used to build a dirty bomb are not that difficult to obtain. They can be found in radiological labs at hospitals where they are used in X-ray technology or to sterilize

### Dirty Bomb in Moscow

In 1995, the only known attempt to attack with a dirty bomb took place in Moscow, Russia. A television station received a tip that a bomb had been planted in a city park. The station's news crew went to the park. They found a partially buried container that contained cesium—a highly radioactive material. The bomb had not been detonated, and Moscow police defused it. It was believed that terrorists from the rebellious Russian state of Chechnya created the bomb.

instruments. They can also be found in meatpacking plants, where they are used to purify meat. Some materials can be found at construction sites where low-level radioactive sensors are used to test welded joints.

In 2004, police in London broke up a ring of suspected terrorists. The group had accumulated ordinary household smoke detectors. Each one contained tiny amounts of nuclear material. London police believed the terrorists hoped to gather enough material from the smoke detectors to make a dirty bomb.

## AL-QAEDA AND DIRTY BOMBS

Al-Qaeda has been linked to several attempts at building a dirty bomb. In 2002, FBI agents broke up a Florida-based cell of Islamic terrorists. Their leader, Jose Padilla, intended to build a dirty bomb. Padilla had traveled to Pakistan, where he met with al-Qaeda leaders.

**Leaky Canisters**

Chemical weapons were first widely used in warfare during World War I. Nearly a century later, those weapons still pose a danger to people. In 2001, the French town of Vimy, which is approximately 90 miles (144.8 km) north of Paris, had to be evacuated. Canisters of mustard gas and phosgene stored at an old weapons dump started leaking. About 12,000 residents of Vimy had to leave their homes for a week until the canisters could be sealed and removed.

*Jose Padilla, center, was caught attempting to build
a dirty bomb for al-Qaeda.*

They gave him $10,000 to obtain the materials
for the bomb. Federal agents received a tip about
Padilla's intentions. They were waiting for him
when he stepped off an airplane in Chicago.

In 2008, Padilla was sentenced to 17 years in prison for conspiracy to commit terrorism.

In 2003, British troops stationed in Afghanistan found diagrams, documents, and information on computer hard drives indicating that al-Qaeda had pursued development of a dirty bomb. "One of these documents spells out in very great detail how to make a dirty bomb," said Vince Cannistraro, former director of counterterrorism for the Central Intelligence Agency (CIA). "The understanding was basically at a fairly advanced physics level. It is a pretty well thought out scenario on how to make the most deadly kind of dirty bomb imaginable."[2]

## POISONING FOOD AND WATER SUPPLY

Authorities are also concerned about the safety of the food supply network in the United States. The idea of attacking an enemy's food supply is not a new one. During World War II, German leaders claimed that British bombers had dropped bags of potato-eating bugs onto Axis croplands in an effort to starve the German people.

Today, more than 100,000 working farms and 150,000 businesses transport, process, package, and sell food in the United States. Each represents a link that could be breached by bioterrorists. Moreover, the United States also imports thousands of tons of food each year. What happens to that food before it reaches U.S. shores is under the authority of food inspectors in foreign countries. The U.S. Food and Drug Administration (FDA) inspects the imported food once it arrives in the United States. But FDA inspectors are stationed at only 90 of the 300 ports of entry in the United States. Critics believe there are too few inspectors to monitor the tons of food that enter the

## Padilla's Dud

Jose Padilla found instructions on how to build a nuclear weapon on the Internet. Padilla thought his weapon would be similar to the nuclear bombs that were dropped on Hiroshima and Nagasaki. When Padilla showed those plans to al-Qaeda leaders in Pakistan, even they thought his intentions were outlandish.

But al-Qaeda leaders thought enough of Padilla's ambitions to pay him $10,000. They urged him to build something smaller—a dirty bomb. Padilla went back to the Internet. He found instructions on how to explode a small quantity of uranium by wrapping it in a common explosive.

After his arrest, scientists examined the terrorist's plans. They concluded that Padilla's dirty bomb would have not have worked. They suggested that uranium is a poor choice for a dirty bomb. It is less radioactive than materials such as cesium and cobalt. These materials, which are used at hospitals, would be much more dangerous in the hands of a terrorist. "I use a 20-pound block of uranium as a doorstop in my office," said King's College London physicist Peter D. Zimmerman. "There is just no significant radiation hazard."[3]

country each day. "What I've found is that the federal inspectors . . . are excellent in their work, but they are understaffed and overworked," said food safety inspector Ed Sherwin.[4]

The 168,000 public water systems in the United States could also be at risk. However, experts note that they are much less vulnerable to terrorism than the food supply. It would take truckloads of toxic chemicals dumped into a public water supply to have an impact on the overall purity of the water. Moreover, the dumping would have to occur in a stream or a system of wells that feed the public water supply. Also, the water would have to be contaminated after it was treated, as the treatment process would likely neutralize the toxins. Environmental Protection Agency (EPA) Administrator Christine Todd Whitman said,

> It would take large amounts of contaminants to threaten the safety of

**Poisoning Rome with Fertilizer**

In 2002, Italian police broke up a terrorist cell that had been making plans to poison Rome's public water system. The suspects were members of an Algerian-based terrorist group. Police found maps of the city's water supply system as well as approximately eight pounds (4 kg) of a chemical that is typically used as a fertilizer. However, experts say that even if the substance had been put into the water network, it would not have caused any damage.

## National Agriculture Biosecurity Center

After the terrorist attacks of 2001, Congress established the National Agricultural Biosecurity Center at Kansas State University. Scientists at the center research biosecurity issues. For example, they have studied methods of safely disposing of animal carcasses infected with biological agents.

This university was selected as the site for the center because Kansas relies heavily on agriculture. The state could be a prime target for terrorists seeking to contaminate the nation's food supply.

*a city water system. . . . We believe it would be very difficult for anyone to introduce the quantities needed to contaminate an entire system.*[5]

Water treatment plants are likely to effectively purify any drinking water that has been contaminated at the source.

<br />

*In the early 2000s, John R. Bolton believed Iran had chemical and biological weapons.*

# ARMED COUNTRIES

*D*espite the international treaties banning biological and chemical warfare, U.S. intelligence officials suspect several nations continue to maintain active programs to develop such weapons. At the top of the list is Iran.

In the early 2000s, Iran became the subject of international scrutiny over its program to develop nuclear weapons. But many political leaders believed the prospect of Iran developing chemical and biological weapons was just as worrisome. "We believe Iran has a covert program to develop and stockpile chemical weapons," said John R. Bolton, a former U.S. undersecretary of state for Arms Control and International Security. "Iran may already have stockpiled blister, blood, choking, and nerve agents—and the bombs and artillery shells to deliver them."[1] Bolton added that Iran is also suspected of developing biological weapons.

If this is the case, Iran would not be the only nation pursuing such weapons. The Henry L. Stimson Center, a Washington-based nonprofit organization that studies peace and security issues, released a study in 2007. The study suggested that at least 21 countries are suspected to have some form of chemical or biological weapons programs. In addition to Iran, these countries included Algeria, China, Cuba, Egypt, Ethiopia, India, Iraq, Israel, Libya, Myanmar, North Korea, Pakistan, Russia, South Africa, South Korea, Sudan, Syria, Taiwan, Vietnam, and the former Yugoslavia.

With the exception of Israel, all of them had signed the 1972 Biological and Toxin Weapons Convention. As of 2008, Egypt, Iraq, Libya, North Korea, and Syria had not signed the 1997 Chemical Weapons Convention.

## LINGERING DANGERS

According to the Stimson Center report, even countries that formerly had biological and chemical weapons programs remain a concern. Among those countries are France, Great Britain, Iraq, and South Africa. In these countries, the resources to develop the weapons remain in place. Laboratories and scientists with expertise in biological and chemical agents are still available. Their programs could be restarted. Some worry that

### Biological Weapons Programs

The Henry L. Stimson Center's report on countries with biological weapons programs in 2007 found the following statistics.

| Country | Status of Program |
| --- | --- |
| Algeria | Suspected, Research |
| China | Likely |
| Cuba | Reported |
| Egypt | Known Research and Development |
| France | Ended |
| Great Britain | Ended |
| Iran | Likely |
| Iraq | Ended |
| Israel | Likely, Research and Development |
| North Korea | Likely |
| Russia | Suspected |
| South Africa | Ended |
| Syria | Seeking |
| United States | Ended |

*President Bill Clinton signed the 1997 Chemical Weapons Convention.*

this could spark a biological and chemical weapons arms race. According to the Stimson Center report, Americans should be most concerned about Russian experts. The report further stated,

> At the height of the Cold War, [the Soviet Union] had
> trained more than 60,000 scientists and engineers in the

*biological weaponry sciences. To date, many of those individuals have not found gainful employment and, therefore, there is a serious risk that their expertise will proliferate to states such as Iran and Syria—states believed to be pursuing offensive biological weapons.*[2]

## Bioweapons Arms Race

Ken Alibek, deputy director of the biological weapons program in the former Soviet Union, came to the United States in 1992. Since then he has warned against an international biological weapons arms race. He said, "I have tried . . . to show how the Soviet Union developed a sophisticated biological warfare program and hid it from the world, but the extent of our achievement shouldn't lead anyone to assume that biological warfare is beyond the grasp of poorer nations."[3]

South Africa is another example. During the nation's apartheid rule, the government had secret plans to attack black opposition leaders with biological weapons. The plans were known as Project Coast. This included spreading diseases throughout the townships populated by blacks. Project Coast also called for killing black leaders by sending envelopes containing anthrax spores and supplying cigarettes tainted with anthrax. The apartheid government in South Africa fell in 1994. A year before the end of apartheid, Prime Minister Frederik W. de Klerk dismantled the country's biological weapons program. Even so, the program had been quite expansive. Many of the components of the program may still remain in the country.

## GREAT BRITAIN AND FRANCE

Great Britain and France, which have long been U.S. allies, both signed the 1997 Chemical Weapons Convention. However, for some years following World War II, both countries are believed to have developed chemical and biological weapons. In 1948, British scientists created a particularly deadly nerve agent known as VX. A few drops of VX on the skin can be lethal. VX eventually found its way into the hands of Saddam Hussein. He may have used it against the Iranians in the 1980s and the Kurds in the 1990s.

In 1988, French President François Mitterrand declared in

"The most characteristic feature of the South African program was the development, testing, and utilization of a wide array of hard-to-trace toxic agents to assassinate 'enemies of the state.'"[4]

—*Gary Ackerman, a biological weapons expert at the Center for Nonproliferation Studies at the Monterey Institute for International Studies in California, describing Project Coast*

*The United States has VX in secured laboratories. Rockets filled with VX are loaded into a container at the Deseret Chemical Depot in Utah.*

a speech to the United Nations that his country suspended its chemical and biological weapons programs. Ken Alibek, deputy director of the biological weapons program in the former Soviet Union, said that in the years leading up to that speech he was aware of at least two biological warfare-related facilities in France as well as one in Germany.

Even after the programs were suspended, their former scientists and workers probably still had some knowledge of the weapons.

## SMALL COUNTRIES

Alibek said that it is likely that other countries have maintained chemical and biological weapons programs. According to Alibek, even small countries with few resources can assemble effective biological and chemical weapons programs. Alibek said,

> Ordinary intelligence and surveillance techniques cannot prove the existence of a biological warfare program. Even the highest resolution satellite imagery can't distinguish between a large pharmaceutical plant and a weapons complex. The only conclusive evidence comes from firsthand information. . . .
>
> Some Western analysts maintain that evidence of biological warfare research

**Chemical Ali**

In the 1980s and 1990s, Saddam Hussein used chemical agents to attack Kurds, a minority group in Iraq. Low-flying jets and helicopters dropped bombs that disseminated clouds of nerve agents and blister agents. These attacks killed as many as 5,000 Kurds in the town of Halabja.

Hussein's chief aide in these attacks was Ali Hassan al-Majid. He was well known for his readiness to use chemical weapons. This earned him the nickname "Chemical Ali."

### Cuba's Biological Weapons Program

For years, U.S. intelligence experts did not believe Cuba maintained a biological weapons program. But in 2002, federal agents announced that they had arrested a Cuban spy, Ana Belen Montes, who had infiltrated the U.S. Defense Intelligence Agency. Posing as an official of the agency, Montes helped draft a 1998 report that said Cuba did not maintain a biological weapons program.

After Montes was arrested, she confessed that she helped cover up evidence of Cuba's biological weapons program. Convicted of treason, Montes could have faced the death penalty. After confessing, she was sentenced to 25 years in prison.

is not proof that viable weapons are being produced. They argue that countries with "low-tech" scientific establishments often can't make weapons or delivery systems matching their ambitions. But even the most primitive biological weapons lab can produce enough of an agent to cripple a major city.[5]

*Dr. Ken Alibek spent 15 years working for the Soviet biological weapons program.*

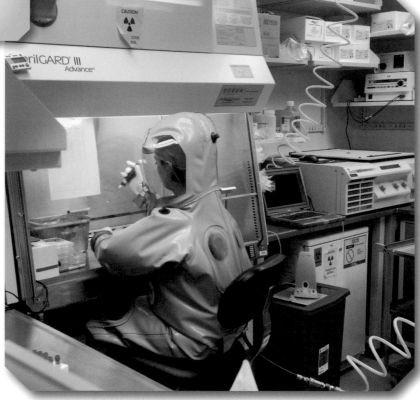

*Scientists study anthrax and other biological agents at Fort Detrick.*

# THE THREAT TO
# AMERICANS

ccording to statistics compiled by
the Centers for Disease Control and
Prevention (CDC) and the Harvard University
Center for Risk Analysis, Americans have a 1 in 322
chance of dying from heart disease. Cancer claims

the lives of 1 in 524 Americans. The chance that an American will die in an auto accident is 1 in 6,579. The likelihood that an American will die in a homicide is 1 in 16,949. And the chance that an American will die in a bioterrorism attack is 1 in 56 million. The statistics seem to suggest that Americans have far greater concerns than falling victim to biological weapons.

## TERRORISTS LACK THE CAPABILITY

Some people insist that biological and chemical weapons are too difficult for terrorists to develop and use effectively. Moreover, once the weapons are deployed, the terrorists can never be sure whether they will reach their targets. Toxic vapors might simply drift away in the wind. Spreading a biological agent over a large urban area requires planes, helicopters, and other equipment that authorities do not believe are

### Dark Scenarios

One of the main critics of the federal government's emphasis on bioterrorism is William R. Clark, a University of California Los Angeles immunology professor and author of *Bracing for Armageddon.* According to Clark, political leaders should be more concerned with conventional weapons falling into the hands of terrorists. Clark said, "Is ricin something that terrorists would use? Maybe. But it's not a contagious agent: only the people who come into contact with it would die. Whether terrorists would find that more effective than a bomb, I don't know. The threat is not zero from bioterrorism. But these dark scenarios where 10 million people die are just not going to happen."[1]

accessible to terrorists. Author and University of California Los Angeles immunology professor William R. Clark said,

> *The more I looked into it, the more I thought, "What are the odds that a terrorist group . . . would be able to create a bioterror weapon?" I began looking into what it takes to really make a successful bioterrorism agent, and I just became very skeptical of this whole thing. The [United States] military gave up bioweapons 30 years ago. They're too undependable; they're too hard to use; they're too hard to make.[2]*

In 2001, Yazid Sufaat spent months trying to create anthrax for al-Qaeda in Afghanistan. He was trained as a biochemist in the United States. But weapons experts point out that there is a big difference between planning to make a weapon and finding the materials and resources to successfully build it. Bruce Ivins

---

**The Threat within the Borders**

Some people claim that U.S. citizens have more to fear within their borders than from foreign countries. Elisa D. Harris, a senior research scholar at the Center for International and Security Studies at the University of Maryland, pointed out that the biggest biological attack in the United States likely came from a member of the U.S. biodefense program—Bruce Ivins.

She wrote, "The United States' own biodefense program has now been tied directly to the deadliest biological attack ever in the country. That alone demonstrates that we need a rigorous, fact-driven assessment of bioweapons threats, both from other counties and from terrorists, domestic and foreign."[3]

*Alleged terrorist Yazid Sufaat attempted to create anthrax for al-Qaeda.*

allegedly developed deadly anthrax spores in a well-equipped laboratory.

To many experts, the idea that al-Qaeda or a similar terrorist group could produce chemical and biological weapons without such resources seems unlikely. Clark points out that in recent years, terrorists have done far more damage and taken more lives with conventional weapons than with biological and chemical agents. Clark said,

> The kind of organization you'd have to put together . . . takes a whole group of people with all kinds of different skills from engineers to meteorologists. That's just not going to happen. You can run an airplane into an office tower, and you get . . . everything you could ever possibly hope for.[4]

## POTENTIAL FOR A PANDEMIC

Several times during the course of human history, plague has wiped out massive numbers of people. However, in modern times, plague pandemics are unlikely. Still, if a terrorist group or an enemy country were able to use plague as a weapon, it could cause widespread pain and death. Unlike anthrax, plague can be spread from person to person. Also, many other biological agents besides plague could be used to start a pandemic.

Most people believe that a pandemic could be especially devastating because, in most nations, it has been a long time since an outbreak has occurred.

*Influenza victims flooded U.S. hospitals in 1918.*

The last serious pandemic in the United States occurred in 1918, when 600,000 people died from the flu. Doctors, hospitals, and ambulance crews have not had to respond to a national medical emergency in nearly a century. As Donald A. Henderson, former director of the U.S. Office of Public Health Preparedness, has said, "The consequences of such an attack would be an epidemic and, in this country . . . we have had little experience in coping with epidemics."[5]

## HOAXES CAN POSE A THREAT

Very few Americans have experienced a real chemical or biological attack. More people have lived through hoaxes that have caused widespread panic. In the years since the 2001 anthrax attacks, many political leaders, journalists, university officials, and others have received envelopes in the mail containing suspicious white powder. Soon after the 2001 attack, several envelopes were sent to Planned Parenthood clinics. In 2008, the Department of Veterans Affairs in Washington DC received a package suspected to contain anthrax. In all cases, the powder has been harmless. It usually turned out to be sugar, flour, talcum powder, or similar substances. The intentions of the

### What Prompts a Threat?

Routinely, the U.S. Homeland Security Department issues a National Threat Advisory, warning Americans when there is a risk of terrorism. The advisory uses a color code, ranging from red for a "severe" threat of terrorism to green for a "low risk."

John Mueller, author of *Overblown: How Politicians and the Terrorism Industry Inflate National Security Threats, and Why We Believe Them,* points out that the Homeland Security department never follows up warnings. The department should explain when the threats that prompted the warnings proved to be baseless, he says. Mueller claims that an explanation of the threats could reduce public fear.

anonymous senders seem to have been to promote fear and panic instead of death.

Even so, police still take all hoaxes very seriously. Typically, an office that receives suspicious mail is evacuated. Then, a hazardous materials team is called in to remove the envelope. Some organizations have endured extensive disruptions to their normal operations. During the 2008 presidential campaign, offices staffed by volunteers for Barack Obama were evacuated after receiving envelopes

### Anthrax Scare

*New York Times* reporter Judith Miller opened a piece of mail filled with suspicious white powder. The incident eventually proved to be a hoax, but the panic Miller felt was real. She later described the event:

*It looked like baby powder. A cloud of hospital white, sweet-smelling powder rose from the letter—dusting my face, sweater and hands. The heavier particles dropped to the floor, falling on my pants and shoes. . . .*

*Calm down, I thought. It's . . . probably a hoax. But when the Times security officers arrived—promptly—I was relieved to see that they were carrying a plastic garbage bag and wearing gloves. . . .*

*Within 20 minutes of the incident, almost a dozen law enforcement officials from almost as many agencies had arrived in the building. . . . While the newsroom floor was evacuated, photographs were made and tests conducted at my desk by police officers, many of them in tan head-to-toe bio-suits with gas masks. . . . I shall never forget the sight of these moon men moving through our normally bustling, now empty newsroom, silent save for the ringing of unanswered phones.[6]*

containing white powder. At Obama's headquarters in Philadelphia, 20 volunteers were evacuated while police and fire authorities inspected the building. They examined the envelope and ultimately declared the threat a hoax. "It turned out to be sugar," said Philadelphia Executive Fire Chief Daniel Williams. "Until you can identify it, it's dangerous."[7]

Because the substances are viewed as dangerous until they can be identified, response teams waste a lot of time, resources, and money on cleaning up and testing during a hoax. Hoaxes also spread real fear among those targeted. ⌐

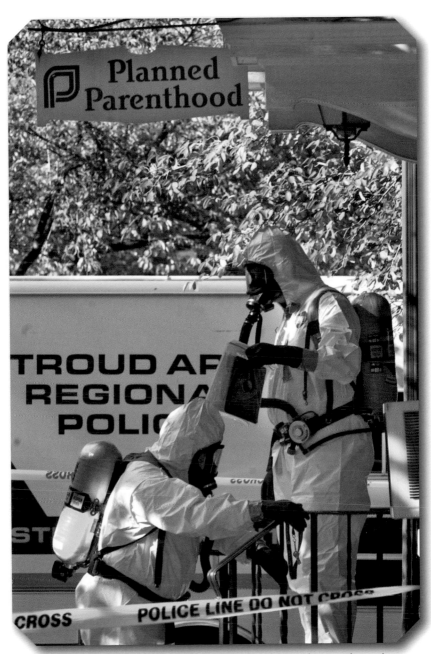

On October 15, 2001, specialists removed items from a Planned Parenthood clinic in Stroudsburg, Pennsylvania, during an anthrax scare.

*ABC studios in Times Square reported the latest news in the 2001 anthrax attacks on October 16.*

# CRITICISM OF RESPONSE TO ATTACKS

ociety still may not know the best way to protect against or handle biological and chemical attacks. Some people claim the steps that have been taken to guard against such attacks have infringed on civil liberties and stalled scientific research. Others worry that, by creating new laboratories, protective measures have actually created new risks.

## IRRESPONSIBLE JOURNALISM

In 2001, news of the anthrax attacks made the front pages of newspapers. It led television news broadcasts for days. Journalism critic Sherry Ricchiardi suggested that government officials and the news media acted irresponsibly during the attacks. She believed the media gave more weight to rumors than to the facts. Ricchiardi noted,

> As the bioterrorism frenzy took hold, factual information was the first casualty. [Countless] contradictions . . . emanated from the White House and other official channels. Mixed messages clouded news conferences and government briefings. As the Bush administration urged Americans to go about their business, the FBI warned that there was evidence of impending new terrorist attacks.[1]

For example, during the fall of 2001, ABC News reported that Iraqi dictator Saddam Hussein may have had a hand in the anthrax attacks. When White House officials challenged the story, ABC News executives defended their reporting. However, the story was later found to be without merit. In the *Oregonian* newspaper in Portland, Oregon, editors published a story headlined, "Nature of Anthrax Doesn't Warrant High Anxiety." As early editions of the newspaper hit the streets, though, the editors decided to pull the story. In later editions, it was replaced with a story suggesting that the anthrax spores mailed to the office of Senator Tom Daschle were more deadly than originally believed.

Some claimed that this type of reporting increased panic during the attacks. Veteran broadcast journalist Dan Rather remarked,

*My own sense is [the anthrax story] has been overcovered,*

### Did Anthrax Lead to War?

In 2001, some reporters and news organizations blamed Iraqi leader Saddam Hussein for the anthrax attacks. Though this turned out not to be true, Hussein's name had been permanently connected to the attacks. Years later, reporters wondered if the anthrax attacks contributed to the media support for the invasion of Iraq in 2003. *Washington Post* columnist Richard Cohen wrote,

*I'm not sure if panic is quite the right word, but it is close enough. Anthrax played a role in my decision to support the Bush administration's desire to take out Saddam Hussein. I linked him to anthrax, which I linked to [September] 11. I was not going to stand by and simply wait for another attack—more attacks. I was going to go to the source, Hussein, and get him before he could get us. As time went on, I became more and more questioning, but I had a hard time backing down from my initial whoop and holler for war.[2]*

*and I worry about that creating exactly what the people who spread this terrible stuff want, which is spreading fear that they hope will result in panic.*[3]

## DESTROYING SPECIMENS

Shortly after the anthrax attacks of 2001, some university administrators ordered their scientific staffs to dispose of all hazardous specimens that were not currently being used in research. Thousands of important samples were destroyed because universities feared that terrorists would steal them. However, most of the samples were frozen and harmless. Also, such actions went beyond federal law. Labs were required to simply register all their specimens with the federal government, not destroy them.

Research scientists criticized the decisions made by the university administrators. Some officials in the federal government also suggested

### Studying the Mutation of Germs

One of the dangers of bio-terrorism is that a germ will be genetically altered to make it resistant to life-saving drugs. For this reason, much scientific research focuses on how the germs can be mutated. To study how a germ has been mutated, scientists often need an early version of the germ to see how it looked before. This is one reason why many scientists have protested the decision by university administrators to dispose of old samples.

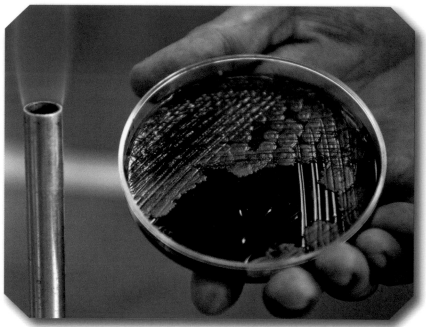

*Many universities destroyed their harmless anthrax samples.*

the administrators were overreacting. They noted that destroying samples could actually slow down the search for vaccines and antidotes. Officials pointed out most scientific research in the United States was conducted by these university labs. Denying them the samples they may need for research could set back their programs by years.

At Iowa State University, all of the school's anthrax specimens were destroyed, including one of the nation's largest collections of the Ames strain, a type of anthrax bacteria. Researchers feared the loss of specimens could seriously damage efforts to find an effective vaccine against the strain. "Obviously, these materials are valuable as research tools, and [for] developing countermeasures should these agents be used as weapons, or if there's an unintentional natural outbreak," said Rachel Levinson, assistant director of the White House Office on Science and Technology Policy.[4]

Still, federal officials strongly enforced the law that all specimens in the labs be registered with the government. At the University of Connecticut, graduate student Tomas Foral was arrested after he failed to follow his professor's orders and destroy two samples of anthrax. Instead, Foral had moved the specimens from one university freezer to another. He was charged with unlawful possession of anthrax since the anthrax had not been registered. He avoided jail in a plea agreement.

### Ivins's Spill

One of the first in a series of accidents in biological research labs occurred in Bruce Ivins's lab during the federal investigation in late 2001. Ivins accidently spilled some anthrax spores. He did not report the incident, as the protocol required.

## New Research Labs

Despite the lost anthrax samples, the number of labs researching anthrax and other biological agents actually increased after 2001. As of August 2008, approximately 14,000 people worked at an estimated 400 laboratories with biological agents. Some people argued that the high number of laboratories and workers increases the risk of accidents. A series of accidents occurred at various labs around the country in the early 2000s. Some people worried that, with so many laboratories for officials to keep track of, they could not properly enforce safety procedures.

In 2006, a worker at a laboratory at Texas A&M University was infected by a bacteria researched there. Three other researchers from the same lab were infected by another bacteria later on. An investigation discovered that standard safety procedures had not been followed. Critics worry that other labs are endangering their workers and the public by not following safety procedures.

**Increased Research**

Following the 2001 anthrax attacks, the field of anthrax research expanded dramatically in just a few years. As of 2008, more than 7,200 researchers were approved to work with anthrax. Additionally, the National Institute of Allergy and Infectious Diseases' budget increased from $270 million in 2002 to $1.75 billion in 2003. Between 2002 and 2008, the United States spent a total of approximately $41 billion on bioterror research.

## HARMLESS SAMPLES

In another case, Buffalo, New York, artist Steve Kurtz was prosecuted for bioterrorism after he obtained samples of harmless bacteria. He had planned to use the bacteria in an avant-garde art exhibit. Kurtz's plans were discovered when his wife died unexpectedly at the couple's home. When paramedics arrived there, they discovered what they regarded as suspicious lab equipment and biological samples. They believed Kurtz's wife had been infected. The paramedics notified the FBI, which seized the materials and held Kurtz for questioning. Later, the samples were found to be harmless and doctors determined that Kurtz's wife died of a heart attack unrelated to any biological agent. Charges of bioterrorism were dropped. But Kurtz was still charged with mail fraud for illegally obtaining the samples.

**Defending the Kurtz Prosecution**

Despite a federal judge's decision to dismiss the charges against Steve Kurtz, prosecutors insisted that the case belonged in court. U.S. Attorney Michael Battle said that, in the wake of the 2001 anthrax attacks, it was in the national interest for the government, as well as universities and private labs, to keep a close watch over biological agents, even if they were harmless. Battle said, "This case has nothing to do with artistic expression and everything to do with public safety."[5]

In 2008, a federal judge dismissed all charges against Kurtz. The artist believes he would not have been arrested had there not been a fear of bioterrorism among political leaders and members of the public. Kurtz said,

> *They tell them, "If there's anything weird, report it." Because probably if it's weird, that means it's suspicious. And if it's suspicious, it's terrorism. They've really managed to ingrain that into people.*[6]

Steve Kurtz became a suspect of bioterrorism when biological samples were found in his home.

President George W. Bush signed legislation
for BioShield on July 21, 2004.

# PREPARING FOR AN ATTACK

ollowing the 2001 terrorist attacks,
President George W. Bush created
the U.S. Homeland Security Department. The
department would coordinate the planning and
carrying out of defensive strategies against terrorism.

This included bioterrorism and chemical attacks. Several agencies already in existence were brought under the Homeland Security umbrella. This allowed them to share information and resources. At the Homeland Security Department, the Directorate of Science and Technology was given the responsibility of guarding against biological and chemical terrorism.

Between 2001 and 2008, the federal government spent nearly $50 billion on biodefense. The money went to fund laboratories, stockpile drugs, and develop vaccines. This money was reserved under the Bioterrorism Preparedness Act of 2001. This act identified chemical and biological warfare as threats against U.S. citizens. As part of the program, President Bush established an initiative known as "Biodefense for the 21st Century." This outlined the steps the federal government would take to help keep Americans safe. Bush warned,

> Armed with a single vial of a biological agent, small groups of fanatics, or failing states, could gain the power to threaten great nations. . . . America, and the entire civilized world, will face this threat for decades to come. We must confront the danger with open eyes, and unbending purpose.[1]

## BioWatch

BioWatch is one of the programs funded under the initiative. BioWatch includes the creation of environmental sensors to detect the presence of biological and chemical weapons in major cities. Some 500 sensor stations in 31 U.S. cities have been created. Each station monitors air quality. Samples are collected daily and taken to laboratories for analysis. The samples are examined for evidence of microorganisms in the air, such as the bacteria that causes anthrax.

However, critics are not convinced that BioWatch is an effective monitoring system. They believe that it would take far more than 500 sensors to effectively react to a bioweapons attack. Calvin Chue is a research scientist at Johns Hopkins University in Baltimore, Maryland. Chue said, "Unless it is a major atmospheric release of large quantities of material, I do not

### BioWatch's Positive Reading

The only time BioWatch sensors are known to have detected evidence of a toxic microorganism occurred in 2003 in Houston, Texas. Two sensing stations detected the bacteria that causes tularemia. For three weeks, biologists tested the samples and monitored the sensor stations while emergency management officials prepared for a full-scale alert. Finally, biologists concluded that the bacteria had occurred in trace amounts. If someone had inhaled the germs, the exposure would not have been enough to cause illness. They suggested the tularemia germs were produced naturally in the environment and not spread by bioterrorists.

think it would be hard at all for BioWatch to miss an attack."[2]

Critics also point out that all the BioWatch sensors are stationed outdoors. So the sensors would miss a chemical or biological weapons attack inside a building. For example, if a terrorist found a way to introduce sarin into the ventilation system of a large office building, BioWatch would not detect it.

Supporters of BioWatch acknowledge that one of the system's big drawbacks is the time it has taken to collect and analyze the samples. In some cases, this has taken up to 36 hours. Critics say that 36 hours is easily enough time for thousands of people to be infected in an attack. In 2009,

### Protecting People in Buildings

Protecting people from an indoor biological or chemical weapon attack is a challenge. In an outdoor attack, the wind can often serve as an effective defense, sweeping a toxic cloud away from a group of people. Indoors, though, the deadly vapors are confined.

In an essay published in *USA Today Magazine*, Michael C. Janus and Robert Rudolph recommended ways to protect people trapped in a building during a bioterrorism attack. They suggested that buildings be outfitted with ventilation control systems that can detect unwanted microorganisms and trap them before they enter the facilities' air circulation systems.

They also suggested steps for sealing off rooms where contamination has occurred. They proposed vacuum devices, which can remove poisoned air. Finally, the authors recommended better evacuation systems for shepherding people outside as quickly as possible.

an improvement in the system was set to begin. This would upgrade sensing stations to provide quick on-site analyses of air samples, making them available to authorities within six hours.

## PROJECT BIOSHIELD

Another initiative is Project BioShield. This project committed nearly $6 billion to medical research to counter the effects of biological and chemical agents. Under Project BioShield, the federal government has funded research for the development of a new anthrax vaccine. It plans to stockpile some 75 million doses in the event of a major anthrax pandemic. Also, Project BioShield has funded research for a new smallpox vaccine.

As with BioWatch, though, the project received some criticism. Some suggest that Project BioShield has been too ambitious. For example, the federal government contracted a drug maker to produce the new anthrax vaccine in five years.

### Project Bioshield and Animal Abuse

People for the Ethical Treatment of Animals (PETA) opposes using animals in laboratory experiments. They have claimed that BioShield programs conduct painful tests on chimpanzees. PETA says that, in researching anthrax and smallpox vaccines, labs have performed bone marrow extractions on the chimps. This procedure requires piercing the bone with a long needle to get to the marrow inside.

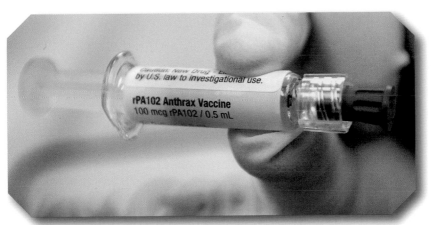

*One BioShield project was to develop and stockpile
a new anthrax vaccine.*

The new vaccine was expected to have fewer side
effects and be more effective than the one currently
in use. However, experts calculated that it would take
at least ten years to develop and test the new vaccine
before it was ready for widespread use.

Ultimately, federal officials cancelled the contract
when the drugmaker failed to meet its deadlines.
Also, the drugs that were produced under the
program are not believed to be highly effective. For
example, under Project BioShield, the Department
of Health and Human Services (HHS) purchased
5 million doses of a drug designed to treat radiation
sickness. Critics claim that this drug is so weak that
it could only work effectively in young children.

In 2007, Carol Linden, a deputy director of HHS, explained, "We are nowhere near where we should be, but it's the nature of the business that developing [drugs and vaccines] . . . takes years and some failures."[3]

## Local Efforts

On a local level, city, county, and state governments have accepted more than $4 billion in federal grants to prepare for bioterror attacks. In many cases, the grants have been used to outfit hazardous-materials response teams. In the aftermath of the 2001 anthrax attacks, authorities assessed the local governments' readiness to respond to bioterror incidents. They concluded that they were not well prepared for such attacks. Monica Shoch-Spana at the University of Pittsburgh's Center for Biosecurity, said,

> *Law enforcement, firefighting, hazardous materials experts and emergency rescue workers, though critical in the aftermath of a chemical or explosive attack, were not professionally equipped to handle an unfolding outbreak.[4]*

In Bucks County, Pennsylvania, local officials obtained $3 million in federal grants. This money bought equipment that would help emergency responders in a bioterrorism event. One such device is an Advanced Portable Detector. It resembles the radar gun a police officer would point at a speeding car. Instead of clocking speeders, the gun detects toxic threats. The Advanced Portable Detector costs $9,600. A more expensive bioterrorism detection device is a $220,000 mobile command center. This bus-sized vehicle is airtight and can be driven into an area where biological or chemical vapors may be. Once it reaches the trouble zone, the bus can have a robot vehicle take air samples. The robot transmits the data back to the command center in the vehicle. Inside the vehicle are television monitors, computers, and telephones.

## Quick Diagnoses

Emergency preparedness officials have realized that most doctors are not trained to recognize the symptoms of the deadly diseases that would be caused by bioterrorism

**Educating Doctors**

William Frist, a physician and former U.S. senator, has pushed to better educate health-care providers about diseases caused by bioterrorism attacks. He said, "Their ability to quickly and correctly recognize diseases with which they have had little, or, more commonly, no direct experience—anthrax, smallpox, plague and other agents . . . will largely determine how many people fall seriously ill and die. We need to better educate medical professionals about infections and organisms that could be used as bioweapons."[5]

## Gathering Data

Doctors and nurses are not the only hospital workers who receive new training to recognize the symptoms of biological and chemical attacks. Clerical workers are also trained to ask questions that could help physicians make their diagnoses.

At Children's Hospital in Boston, admissions workers who routinely ask for basic information have been trained to ask additional questions. For example, they ask whether the patients work around chemicals or whether they may have come into contact with suspicious substances.

It is hoped that this data can help doctors recognize a trend and take action. For example, if several employees from the same post office come into the hospital with similar symptoms, public health authorities can be called to investigate.

strikes. Hospitals have started training physicians to recognize the symptoms of anthrax, smallpox, nerve agents, and various other poisons. Assisting doctors is the Rapid Syndrome Validation Project, an Internet-based computer network. The system compares a person's symptoms against those recorded in a national database. This lets doctors make more accurate diagnoses.

Proponents of the system hope to have it installed in all hospital emergency rooms in the United States. They hope to decrease the time it takes to make a diagnosis to a few minutes or hours. "Those first few hours . . . are difficult," conceded Jeffrey Koplan, former director of the U.S. Centers for Disease Control and Prevention (CDC). "No one is going to walk in and say, 'Oh, this must be anthrax' when someone comes in with a cough and a cold and a headache."[6]

During the 2001 anthrax attacks, Washington-area postal workers stood in line to be examined at Columbia General Hospital.

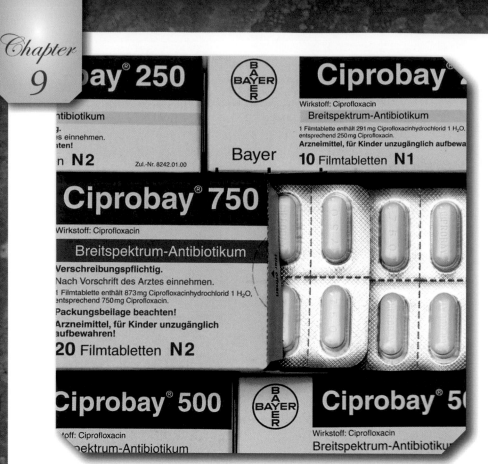

*Ciprobay antibiotics treat anthrax in humans.*

# IN THE WAKE
## OF AN ATTACK

lthough a biological or chemical weapons attack is rare, governments still need to be prepared. They have many plans in place for helping injured or infected citizens. Individuals can also learn how to protect and care for themselves in the wake of an attack.

## ANTHRAX ANTIDOTE

It is possible to survive an anthrax attack, as there is an effective antidote. Ciproflaxin, commonly known as Cipro, treats the symptoms of anthrax. It can also be taken before exposure to the anthrax bacteria as a preventive measure. In the event of an anthrax attack, the government has promised to make Cipro available to those at risk. People can also obtain doses from their doctors. However, Cipro presents many unpleasant side effects, such as nausea.

An anthrax vaccine has also been available since the 1940s. Since anthrax is still a rare disease in humans, the vaccine generally is not administered. Until 1989, only 68,000 Americans had been vaccinated against anthrax. The only Americans who routinely receive the vaccine are members of the armed services who are heading into war zones overseas.

**Washing Hands**

Each day, the U.S. Postal Service delivers 700 million pieces of mail. It is impossible for authorities to check each piece of mail for evidence of a biological agent. If people are concerned about being contaminated, officials at the U.S. Centers for Disease Control and Prevention (CDC) suggest they wash their hands after opening the mail.

## Eating Healthfully Kills Bacteria

Certain foods enhance the growth of bacteria in the body. They include milk products and anything rich in sugar or caffeine. Starches, such as bread and pasta, also fall into this category because the body breaks them down into sugars. Alcohol also contains a lot of sugar. Therefore, people whose diets are rich in caffeine, milk, starch, and especially sugar are likely to get more ill in a biological weapons attack than people who avoid such foods.

Diets high in vegetables and fiber help ward off bacterial growth. Also, people who drink plenty of water and juice are constantly flushing bacteria from their systems. Therefore, people who eat healthfully and drink a lot of water have built up some natural defenses against bacterial agents.

While research continues, the anthrax antidote is one of many drugs that can be effective in biological and chemical weapons attacks. Common antibiotics are used to treat tularemia and plague. In 2007, the Food and Drug Administration (FDA) approved a new version of the smallpox vaccine for human use. The agency cautioned, though, that it need not be administered unless the disease resurfaces as a threat. Still, the Centers for Disease Control and Prevention (CDC) has stockpiled nearly 200 million doses and is prepared to distribute them should the need arise.

## Nerve Gas Antidotes

No drug exists that can protect against nerve gas or other chemical weapons. People in the path of a chemical agent should evacuate the area. Military personnel facing attack by chemical weapons usually

*New York Mayor Michael R. Bloomberg received
a smallpox vaccination in 2003.*

have oxygen masks and other protective clothing
and equipment. However, some drugs can help
save the lives of people who have inhaled poison
gases. Military personnel have antidote kits they
can use if they are exposed to nerve agents. Two
drugs, atropine and pralidoxime, are effective in
slowing down the central nervous system. This can
delay and diffuse the effects of nerve gases on the
body. However, to be effective, the drugs have to be
administered within minutes of the poisonous vapors

reaching the victim's lungs. A medical professional injects the drugs into the victim's thigh.

In the town of Newton, Massachusetts, police and fire units were equipped with nerve-gas antidote kits. Mayor David Cohen explained,

*We believe that the risk to Newton is small but . . . we have to take even that small threat very seriously today. In dealing with this sensitive topic, we have been very careful to respond prudently. This is prudent and not an over-response.*[1]

---

**Hazmat Suits**

Before emergency responders enter an area where biological and chemical agents may have been deployed, they put on hazardous materials suits. The suits are also known as hazmat suits. They provide three levels of protection: A, B, and C.

Level A suits offer full protection. They are also known as "moon suits" because they resemble the suits worn by astronauts. They are airtight so that toxic vapors cannot get in. Tanks supply air to the worker. The suits are so heavy and cumbersome that they cannot be worn for more than 15 or 20 minutes at a time. Inside the suit, a worker may sweat so much that his or her mask will fog up. Nevertheless, these suits offer the best protection against nerve gas.

Level B suits are not airtight, although the responder does wear an oxygen mask to protect against breathing toxic vapors. Level B suits are regarded as sufficient for investigating anthrax cases. However, many emergency responders insist on Level A protection when confronting any suspected biological agent.

Level C protection usually includes oxygen masks. The emergency responders also wear heavy gloves and boots taped to coveralls so that stray particles cannot fall inside their clothing.

## SURVIVING A DIRTY BOMB ATTACK

The first line of defense for someone infected by a dirty bomb may be a shower with soap or diluted household bleach. Many hospitals are equipped with decontamination showers. These showers are much stronger than ordinary household showers. Hazardous materials teams are often equipped with portable decontamination showers that can be set up at the site. In the past, the showers have been used at the scene of a chemical plant accident or similar mishap. But they could also be used to cleanse bodies after a dirty bomb attack.

Of course, a shower can only wash the material off the skin. Victims of a dirty bomb attack are likely to inhale the poisonous vapors. One of the few drugs available as an antidote for dirty bomb victims is potassium iodide, or KI. During a dirty bomb attack, radioactive iodine is released into the air. If the radioactive iodine

### Duct Tape and Plastic

In the months after the 2001 anthrax attacks, the U.S. Homeland Security Department issued a set of guidelines for people who feared that biological or chemical agents could seep into their homes. They suggested that people seal their windows and doors with plastic sheets and duct tape.

At first, people flocked to hardware stores to stock up on duct tape and other supplies. But soon scientists and others disputed those recommendations. They claimed that no matter how much duct tape was used, no home could ever be made airtight and, therefore, 100 percent protected against intrusive bacteria.

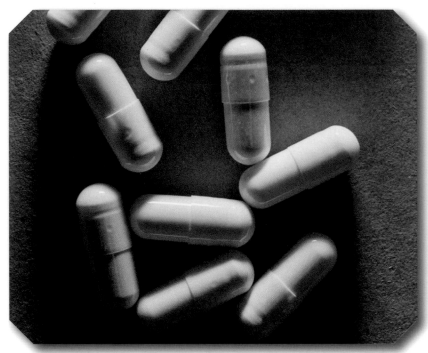

*Potassium iodide capsules can prevent radioactive iodine from causing cancer in the thyroid gland.*

is ingested, it can cause cancer in the thyroid gland. When taken within four hours of contamination, KI floods the thyroid gland with nonradioactive iodine. This prevents the uptake of radioactive iodine into the gland. However, KI is effective in preventing cancer in the thyroid gland only. Other parts of the body are not protected.

## Panic Is a Concern

In the event of any chemical or biological weapons attack, national security experts fear panic the most. If a dirty bomb exploded, for example, emergency rooms would soon be filled with hundreds or even thousands of people. The crowds would demand to use the few decontamination showers that may be available. Graham Allison, former assistant secretary of defense, says chaos would likely ensue:

> [People] probably haven't been well-informed. They would quickly go to a web site to try to see what they could learn about it. Some people would go out and buy a book about nuclear terrorism and other people would take sodium iodide, thinking, "I heard that that had something to do with this or that." But there would be general confusion . . . given on the one hand the absence of an effective education process for people, and on the other the desire not to know too much about this.[2]

## Remaining Alert

Despite the fact that an attack is unlikely, biological and chemical weapons are still a source of concern. There will always be the fear that radical groups will find ways to explode a dirty bomb, spread anthrax, or release sarin vapors into a closed environment. Political leaders, military leaders, law enforcement officials, and scientists tackle the problem on several fronts. They must keep chemical and biological agents out of the hands of enemies. They must make sure emergency measures are in place should an attack occur. They must continue developing antidotes and vaccines. At the same time, they must ensure that the level of their response is appropriate to the threat, so panic stays at bay. ⌐

*During a bioterrorism preparedness exercise, emergency responders use decontamination showers.*

# TIMELINE

| ca. 500 BCE | 1770s | 1899 |
| --- | --- | --- |
| During the Peloponnesian War, allies of the Spartans fling torches that burn sulfur and pitch over the walls of an Athenian fort. | During the American Revolution, the British leave the bodies of smallpox victims, hoping they will infect the colonists. | Most European countries sign the first Hague Peace Conventions. |

| 1925 | 1936 | 1940s |
| --- | --- | --- |
| World leaders sign the Geneva Protocol, outlawing chemical and biological warfare. | Italian troops invade Ethiopia, using chemical weapons spread by airplanes. | The Nazis employ chemical agents to kill millions of concentration camp inmates. |

## 1907

The second Hague Peace Conventions reinforce the ban on chemical and biological warfare in combat.

## 1915

The Germans first use chlorine gas against French and Canadian soldiers in Belgium.

## 1918

An influenza pandemic kills 600,000 people in the United States.

## 1945

An anthrax epidemic in Iran kills 1 million sheep.

## 1969

On November 25, President Nixon suspends the U.S. chemical and biological weapons program.

## 1972

More than 100 nations sign the Biological and Toxin Weapons Convention.

# TIMELINE

## 1980–1988

During the Iraq-Iran War, the Iraqis are believed to have used chemical weapons against Iranian soldiers.

## 1995

A television news crew in Moscow, Russia, finds an undetonated dirty bomb in a public park.

## 1997

The Chemical Weapons Convention takes effect. It outlaws biological and chemical weapons.

## 2004

Ukrainian political leader Viktor Yushchenko survives an assassination attempt of poisoning by dioxin.

## 2006

A task force learns of a discrepancy in evidence turned over to investigators by Bruce Ivins.

## 2001

On September 19, Robert Stevens opens a letter containing anthrax spores. He dies 16 days later.

## 2002

On October 26, Russian soldiers use what may have been nerve gas against a group of terrorists. A total of 129 people die.

## 2003

British troops in Afghanistan uncover documents suggesting that al-Qaeda planned to build a dirty bomb.

## 2007

A Henry L. Stimson Center report suggests that at least nine countries are developing chemical and biological weapons.

## 2008

Bruce Ivins commits suicide on July 28.

# Essential Facts

## At Issue

❖ Since the 2001 anthrax attacks, bioterrorism has been an area of increased concern, although many question the likelihood of such an attack.

❖ Programs such as BioShield, BioWatch, and the Rapid Syndrome Validation Project aim to protect Americans against a biological or chemical attack. However, some people doubt the effectiveness of these systems and believe that the United States is not equipped to handle an attack.

❖ According to a 2007 Henry L. Stimson Center report, countries suspected to have some type of biological or chemical weapons programs are Algeria, China, Cuba, Egypt, Ethiopia, India, Iran, Iraq, Israel, Libya, Myanmar, North Korea, Pakistan, Russia, South Africa, South Korea, Sudan, Syria, Taiwan, Vietnam, and the former Yugoslavia.

❖ Many countries that produced chemical or biological weapons in the past still have the institutions and research to begin producing the weapons again.

## Critical Dates

**Fifth century BCE**
The first known instance of chemical warfare occurred during the Peloponnesian War.

**July 29, 1899**
At the first Hague Peace Conventions, most European countries promised not to use chemical or biological weapons in warfare.

**October 18, 1907**
The second Hague Peace Conventions reinforced the agreement made in 1899.

**1915–1918**
Beginning in 1915, the German army used chlorine and mustard gas against the Allies during World War I.

**June 17, 1925**
The Geneva Protocol outlawed chemical and biological warfare.

**1939–1945**
In World War II, the Germans used gas to murder millions of Jews and other prisoners in concentration and death camps.

**November 25, 1969**
U.S. President Richard M. Nixon suspended the country's biological and chemical weapons program.

**April 10, 1972**
The Biological and Toxin Weapons Convention was signed by more than 100 nations.

**April 29, 1997**
The Chemical Weapons Convention prohibited the development, production, stockpiling, and use of chemical weapons and created a system for inspection.

**September 2001**
A series of anthrax attacks caused panic in the United States. Five people died of anthrax.

## Quotes

"If the objective is to inflict mass death and panic on a mixed population . . . emerging bioweapons offer remarkable potential."—*Professor Barry Kellman*

"I began looking into what it takes to really make a successful bioterrorism agent, and I just became very skeptical of this whole thing. The [United States] military gave up bioweapons 30 years ago. They're too undependable; they're too hard to use; they're too hard to make."—*Professor William R. Clark*

# ADDITIONAL RESOURCES

## SELECT BIBLIOGRAPHY

Baker, Nicholson. *Human Smoke: The Beginnings of World War II, the End of Civilization*. New York: Simon & Schuster, 2008.

Harding, Kyle. "Biological Weapons." Washington: Henry L. Stimson Center. 23 May 2007 <http://www.stimson.org/?SN=CT200705231269>.

Ricchiardi, Sherry. "The Anthrax Enigma." *American Journalism Review*. Dec. 2001 < http://www.ajr.org/Article.asp?id=2372>.

Weintraub, Pamela. *Bioterrorism: How to Survive the 25 Most Dangerous Biological Weapons*. New York: Citadel Press, 2002.

## FURTHER READING

Dudley, William. *Biological Warfare: Opposing Viewpoints*. Farmington Hills, MI: Greenhaven Press, 2004.

Jones, Simon. *World War I: Gas Warfare Tactics and Equipment*. Oxford, UK: Osprey Publishing, 2007.

Judson, Karen. *Chemical and Biological Warfare*. New York: Benchmark Books, 2004.

Koestler-Grack, Rachel A. *The Department of Homeland Security*. New York: Chelsea House, 2007.

## WEB LINKS

To learn more about biological and chemical warfare, visit ABDO Publishing Company online at **www.abdopublishing.com**. Web sites about biological and chemical warfare are featured on our Book Links page. These links are routinely monitored and updated to provide the most current information available.

## For More Information

For more information on this subject, contact or visit the following organizations.

**United States Holocaust Memorial Museum**
100 Raoul Wallenberg Place, Southwest
Washington, DC 20024–2126
202-488-0400
www.ushmm.org
The muscum features many exhibits that explain the use of chemical and biological weapons during World War II, including the gas used by the Nazis to exterminate millions of Jews and other concentration camp inmates.

**U.S. Centers for Disease Control and Prevention**
Office of Communication, Building 16, D-42
1600 Clifton Road, Northeast, Atlanta, GA 30333
800-311-3435
www.cdc.gov
The federal government's chief public health agency monitors trends in diseases and would be the first to respond to a bioterrorism emergency. The agency maintains a large repository of drugs and other medical supplies that can be rushed to the scene of a biological weapons attack.

**U.S. Department of Homeland Security**
245 Murray Lane, Southwest, Washington, DC 20528
202-282-8000
www.dhs.gov
The department is responsible for alerting Americans to threats involving biological or chemical weapons. It also works closely with local emergency responders, making financial aid available to help them buy hazardous materials suits, vehicles, and other equipment.

# GLOSSARY

**agent**
A substance that causes an effect.

**Agent Orange**
A chemical composed of dioxin, used by the U.S. military during the Vietnam War to remove the leaves from trees.

**anthrax**
A deadly disease spread by bacteria; it mostly afflicts farm animals that ingest contaminated grasses.

**bacteria**
Microscopic organisms that infect living cells.

**central nervous system**
A bodily system composed of the brain and the spinal cord. It is responsible for sending instructions to all parts of the body.

**chlorine**
A familiar household chemical used to clean swimming pool water; it is very toxic in its gaseous form and can cause burning pain in the eyes and throat and spasms in the chest.

**cholera**
A disease that is spread by bacteria and attacks the gastrointestinal system.

**dirty bomb**
A device that can spread radioactive material over a widespread area.

**DNA**
Short for deoxyribonucleic acid, DNA is a molecule that stores information that determines the hereditary properties of organisms.

**epidemic**
A disease affecting many people at once and spreading across the population.

**gastrointestinal system**
A bodily system composed of the stomach and the intestines. It is responsible for digesting food.

**mustard gas**
> A blister agent that causes severe irritation to the eyes, the skin, and the lungs. It is composed of sulfur and other chemicals.

**pandemic**
> An outbreak of disease affecting a widespread area.

**radioactive**
> Used to describe a substance that emits rays of energy as particles from unstable atoms.

**sarin**
> A nerve agent that shuts down the central nervous system, capable of causing death within 15 minutes.

**smallpox**
> A viral infection that caused some 500 million deaths before it was eliminated through vaccinations.

**vaccine**
> Medicine that makes the body immune to a particular disease.

**virus**
> A microscopic disease-carrying organism that is passed from living thing to living thing.

# SOURCE NOTES

**Chapter 1. The Hunt for the Anthrax Killer**
1. Amanda Ripley. "The Hunt for the Anthrax Killers." *Time Canada*. 5 Nov. 2001. 24.
2. Barry Kellman. "Bioviolence: A Growing Threat." *The Futurist*. May-June 2008. 26.
3. Joby Warrick. "Trail of Odd Anthrax Cells Led FBI to Army Scientist." *Washington Post*. 27 Oct. 2008. A-1.
4. Joby Warrick, Marilyn W. Thompson, and Nelson Hernandez. "A Scientist's Quiet Life Took a Darker Turn." *Washington Post*. 2 Aug. 2008. A-1.
5. Amanda Ripley. "The Anthrax Files." *Time Canada*. 18 Aug. 2008. 18.

**Chapter 2. Deadly Weapons**
1. David Cloud, and Nicholas Kulish. "U.S. Fears Four Nations Hold Smallpox." *Wall Street Journal*. 6 Nov. 2002. 1.
2. Ann Davis. "Toxic Cloud: New Alarms Heat Up Debate on Publicizing Chemical Risks—Environmentalists Air Data That Plants Fear Will Make Them Targets of Terrorists." *Wall Street Journal*. 30 May 2002. A-1.
3. Michael Wines. "Hostage Toll in Russia Over 100; Nearly All Deaths Linked to Gas." *New York Times*. 28 Oct. 2002. A-1.
4. Ibid.

**Chapter 3. Centuries of Killing**
1. Garance Franke-Ruta. "George Washington's Bioterrorism Strategy." *Washington Monthly*. Dec. 2001. 54.
2. Anthony Hossack. "Memories and Diaries: The First Gas Attack." Charles Benjamin Purdom, ed.. *Everyman at War*. London: J.M. Dent, 1930. Firstworldwar.com. 18 Feb. 2009 <http://www.firstworldwar.com/diaries/firstgasattack.htm>.
3. Nicholson Baker. *Human Smoke: The Beginnings of World War II, the End of Civilization*. New York: Simon & Schuster, 2008. 62–63.
4. "The Living Weapon." *American Experience*. 15 Dec. 2006. PBS.org. 19 Feb. 2009 <http://www.pbs.org/wgbh/amex/weapon/filmmore/pt.html>.
5. Ibid.

### Chapter 4. Biological and Chemical Terrorism

1. "Dirty Bomb." *Nova.* 25 Feb. 2003. PBS.org. 19 Feb. 2009 <http://www.pbs.org/wgbh/nova/transcripts/3007_dirtybom. html>.
2. Ibid.
3. Associated Press. "Bomb Would Have Been a Dud, Scientists Say." *New York Times.* 10 June 2004. A-25.
4. E.J. Mundell. "U.S. Food Safety: The Import Alarm Keeps Sounding." *U.S. News and World Report.* 15 Jan. 2008. US News. com. 19 Feb. 2009 <http://health.usnews.com/usnews/health/ healthday/080115/us-food-safety-the-import-alarm-keeps -sounding.htm>.
5. Wendi Hope King. "Bioterrorism May Pose Threat to Water Supplies." *Water & Wastes Digest.* Dec. 2001. wwdmag.com. 19 Feb. 2009 <http://www.wwdmag.com/Bioterrorism-May-Pose-Threat -to-Water-Supplies-article2809>.

### Chapter 5. Armed Countries

1. John R. Bolton. "Iran's Continuing Pursuit of Weapons of Mass Destruction." Testimony before the U.S. House International Relations Committee, Subcommittee on the Middle East and Central Asia. 24 June 2004. MERLN.ndu.edu. 23 Feb. 2009 <http://merln.ndu.edu/archivepdf/iran/State/33909.pdf>.
2. Kyle Harding. "Biological Weapons." Washington: Henry L. Stimson Center. 23 May 2007. Stimson.org. 23 Feb. 2009 <http://www.stimson.org/?SN-CT200705231269>.
3. Ken Alibek. *Biohazard.* New York: Random House, 1999. 277–278.
4. Joby Warrick. "Biotoxins Fall Into Private Hands: Global Risk Seen in South African Poisons." *Washington Post.* 21 Apr. 2003. A-1.
5. Ken Alibek. *Biohazard.* New York: Random House, 1999. 277–278.

## SOURCE NOTES CONTINUED

### Chapter 6. The Threat to Americans

1. Matt Palmquist. "Bioterror in Context." *Miller-McCune*. 19 May 2008. Miller-McCune.com. 18 Feb. 2009 <http://www.miller-mccune.com/article/355>.

2. Ibid.

3. Elisa D. Harris. "The Killers in the Lab." *New York Times*. 11 Aug. 2008. NYT.com. 13 Feb. 2009 <http://www.nytimes.com/2008/08/12/opinion/12harris.html?scp=10&sq=biological%20weapons%20defense&st=cse>.

4. Matt Palmquist. "Bioterror in Context." *Miller-McCune*. 19 May 2008. Miller-McCune.com. 18 Feb. 2009 <http://www.miller-mccune.com/article/355>.

5. Pamela Weintraub. *Bioterrorism: How to Survive the 25 Most Dangerous Biological Weapons*. New York: Citadel Press, 2002. 4.

6. Judith Miller. "Fear Hits Newsroom in a Cloud of Powder." *New York Times*. 14 Oct. 2001. 1-B.

7. Anthony R. Wood. "Obama Headquarters Evacuated After Threat." *Philadelphia Inquirer*. 15 Oct. 2008. philly.com. 18 Feb. 2009 <http://www.philly.com/philly/news/pennsylvania/20081015_Obama_headquarters_evacuated_after_threat.html>.

### Chapter 7. Criticism of Response to Attacks

1. Sherry Ricchiardi. "The Anthrax Enigma." *American Journalism Review*. Dec. 2001. AJR.com. 18 Feb. 2009 < http://www.ajr.org/Article.asp?id=2372>.

2. Richard Cohen. "Our Forgotten Panic." *The Washington Post*. 22 July 2004. washingtonpost.com 18 Feb. 2009 < http://www.washingtonpost.com/wp-dyn/articles/A4328-2004Jul21.html>.

3. Sherry Ricchiardi. "The Anthrax Enigma." *American Journalism Review*. Dec. 2001. AJR.com. 18 Feb. 2009 < http://www.ajr.org/Article.asp?id=2372>.

4. Diana Kean Schemo. "After 9-11, Universities are Destroying Biological Agents." *New York Times*. 17 Dec. 2002. A-20.

5. Andrew Z. Galarneau. "A Life Turned Upside Down: Steve Kurtz's Art Gained Wide Audience as FBI Came Knocking." *Buffalo News*. 4 Apr. 2008.
6. Ibid.

**Chapter 8. Preparing for an Attack**

1. "Biodefense for the 21ˢᵗ Century." White House news release. 28 Apr. 2004. whitehouse.gov. 18 Feb. 2009 <http://www.whitehouse.gov/homeland/20040430.html>.
2. Ted Birdis, Associated Press. "Is Biowatch Testing Your Air? The Program Sniffs the Air in 31 Cities for Bioterror Contaminants. How Well It Works Is Still Debated." *Philadelphia Inquirer*. 15 Nov. 2003. A-7.
3. Angie C. Marek. "A Meager Yield from BioShield; A Federal Effort to Protect the Public from Bioterrorism Isn't Off to a Strong Start." *U.S. News & World Report*. 26 Mar. 2007. US News.com. 19 Feb. 2009 <http://www.usnews.com/usnews/news/articles/070318/26vaccine.htm>.
4. Monica Shoch-Spana. "Bioterrorism: U.S. Public Health and a Secular Apocalypse." *Anthropology Today*. Oct. 2004. 9.
5. Bill Frist. *When Every Moment Counts: What You Need to Know About Bioterrorism from the Senate's Only Doctor*. Lanham, MD: Rowman & Littlefield Publishers, Inc., 2002. 162.
6. Lawrence K. Altman. "Disease Experts Struggle to Help Doctors Discern the Early Flu from Early Anthrax." *New York Times*. 1 Nov. 2001. B-10.

**Chapter 9. In the Wake of an Attack**

1. Christopher Rowland. "City Will Stock Nerve-Gas Antidote Kits to Help Protect Police, Firefighters." *Boston Globe*. 22 Sept. 2002. 1.
2. "Dirty Bomb." *Nova*. 25 Feb. 2003. PBS.org. 19 Feb. 2009 <http://www.pbs.org/wgbh/nova/dirtybomb/allison.html>.

# INDEX

# ABOUT THE AUTHOR

Hal Marcovitz is a former newspaper reporter who has written more than 100 books for young readers. In 2005, *Nancy Pelosi*, his biography of House Speaker Nancy Pelosi, was named in *Booklist* magazine's list of recommended feminist books for young readers. As a journalist, he won three Keystone Press Awards, the highest award for newspaper reporting presented by the Pennsylvania Newspaper Association.

# PHOTO CREDITS

Kenneth Lambert/AP Images, cover; C. Todd Sherman/AP Images, 6; FBI/AP Images, 8; Rob Carr/AP Images, 15; U.S. Army /AP Images, 16, 97 (bottom); Misha Japaridze/AP Images, 23, 99; Elaine Thompson/AP Images, 25; Library of Congress, 26, 96; Department of Defense/AP Images, 32; Efrem Lukatsky/ AP Images, 35, 98 (bottom); Travis Morisse/AP Images, 36; Alan Diaz/AP Images, 40; Susan Montoya Bryan/AP Images, 45; Charles Dharapak/AP Images, 46; Wilfredo Lee/AP Images, 49, 98 (top); Chuck Sprague/AP Images, 51; Doug Mills/AP Images, 55; Sam Yu/AP Images, 56; AP Images, 59; National Museum of Health/AP Images, 61, 97 (top); David Kidwell/AP Images, 65; Tina Fineberg/AP Images, 66; Victor R. Caivano/AP Images, 70; David Duprey/AP Images, 75; Evan Vucci/AP Images, 76; Benjamin Sklar/AP Images, 81; Ken Cedeno/AP Images, 85; Michael Sohn/AP Images, 86; Joseph Reyes/AP Images, 89; Christopher Pfuhl/AP Images, 92; Damian Dovarganes/AP Images, 95